# RED
## FORT

**DORLING KINDERSLEY**
London, New York, Munich,
Melbourne and Delhi

| | |
|---|---|
| **Head of Publishing** | Aparna Sharma |
| **Art Director** | Shefali Upadhyay |
| **Design Manager** | Arunesh Talapatra |
| **Designers** | Ivy Roy, Neerja Rawat |
| **Editors** | Dipali Singh, |
| | Kingshuk Ghoshal, |
| | Suchismita Banerjee |
| **Production Manager** | Pankaj Sharma |
| **DTP Designers** | Jagtar Singh, Dheeraj Arora, |
| | Harish Aggarwal |
| **Photographer** | Sanjay Austa |

First published in India in 2008
by Dorling Kindersley (India) Pvt. Limited
in association with Penquin Book India (P) Ltd.,
11, Community Centre, Panchsheel Park, New Delhi - 110017
Copyright © 2008 Dorling Kindersley (India) Pvt. Limited

ISBN 978-0-14-306555-5

Printed and bound in
Gopsons Papers Ltd., Noida, India

Discover more at
**www.dk.com**

Discover more at
**www.penguinbooksindia.com**

# RED
# FORT

# Citadel of Power

The Red Fort (Lal Qila) in Delhi is the paramount symbol of Mughal grandeur. Made of red sandstone, this fort, now a UNESCO World Heritage Site, epitomizes the ingenuity and creativity of Mughal architecture and aesthetics. Located between the river Yamuna and Shahjahanabad (the seventh city of Delhi), the fort contained an array of palaces and pavilions, set in ornamental gardens. Emperor Shah Jahan commissioned the construction of the fort in the early 17th century. Under the supervision of master-architect Makramat Khan, it was completed in nine years. It is said that the construction of the fort cost over ten million rupees. In 1648, the emperor and his entourage entered the fort amidst ceremonial drumbeats and celebrations. Shahjahanabad replaced

◈ **IMPERIAL CAPITAL**
*Delhi was the administrative centre of the Mughals from 1648–1857.*

Agra as the imperial capital. Reflecting the Mughal love of opulence, brocades, curtains, carpets, cushions, and gem-encrusted walls beautified the palaces and pavilions, flowers bloomed in the gardens, and water from the river Yamuna fed the many fountains and channels. The river flowed along the eastern wall of the fort. The decline of the Mughals coincided with attacks on the city and the vandalizing of the palaces. After 1857, the British forces demolished many buildings within the fort and then occupied it. In 1947, the Red Fort was chosen as the site of a momentous event – the first hoisting of independent India's flag. This historic fort has been a spectator to India in the making, resonating with event-filled chapters in the history of the nation.

## The Mughal Emperors

The conquest of north India by Babur heralded the establishment of the Mughal dynasty. One of the greatest empires in the history of the Indian subcontinent, the Mughals ruled over 100 million subjects at the zenith of their power. Their government was based on a centralized administrative system. After two centuries of stability, the Mughal empire began to decline by the early 18th century.

- 1526 The Mughal empire is founded by **Babur**, with Agra as its chief city.

- 1530 **Humayun** accedes to the throne.

- 1555–1605 Reign of **Akbar**.

- 1605–1627 Reign of **Jahangir**.

- 1628 **Shah Jahan** accedes to the throne.

- 1648 Shah Jahan moves his capital from Agra to **Shahjahanabad**. Construction of **Red Fort** completed.

- 1658–1707 Reign of **Aurangzeb**.

- 1739 **Nadir Shah** of Persia (modern-day Iran) invades Delhi.

- 1838 **Bahadur Shah Zafar**, the last Mughal emperor, comes to the throne.

- 1857 **First War of Independence** is fought. The British East India Company quells uprising and its army occupies Red Fort.

- 1858 The British forces exile Bahadur Shah Zafar to Myanmar, **ending Mughal rule.**

# A Fort's History

The Red Fort, a testimony to the power of the Mughals, was a miniature city, east of the city of Shahjahanabad. During Emperor Shah Jahan's reign, the fort was known as Qila-i-Mubarak (Auspicious Citadel). Later, it was called the Lal Qila (Red Fort). After the Mughals, the fort was occupied by the British and, till 2003, by the Indian army.

## The age of great architecture

When Prince Khurram became emperor, he took the title of Shah Jahan (King of the World). Shah Jahan, much like his grandfather Akbar, was a patron of the arts and his reign witnessed the golden age of Mughal architecture. Besides the Red Fort, his legacy includes the grand Jama Masjid in Delhi; the Shah Jahan Mosque in Sind, Pakistan; and the Moti Masjid (Pearl Mosque), Wazir Khan Mosque, sections of the Lahore Fort, and the Shalimar Gardens in Lahore, Pakistan. In Agra, he built sizeable parts of the Agra Fort as well as the magnificent Taj Mahal.

**TAJ MAHAL**
*Considered one of the Seven Wonders of the world, the Taj Mahal was built under Shah Jahan's patronage. This exquisite memorial for his wife, Mumtaz Mahal, is faced with marble and is perfectly symmetric.*

**JAMA MASJID**
*Built in 1656 by Emperor Shah Jahan, the three-domed Jama Masjid in Delhi is one of the finest mosques in India.*

## INVASIONS AND PLUNDER

Marauders from regions near Delhi took advantage of Mughal vulnerability in the 18th century. In 1739, Emperor Nadir Shah of Persia reached Delhi. It is said that, angered by a rumour of his death, he ordered the slaughter of the local people. Thousands were killed, parts of the city were set on fire, and the Red Fort was pillaged. The Peacock Throne, the royal treasury, and precious jewels and manuscripts were plundered. These events were repeated when the Afghan chief, Ahmed Shah Durrani, attacked Delhi.

**SHAH JAHAN**
*This 17th-century painting shows Emperor Shah Jahan holding court.*

# Modern times

After the First War of Independence in 1857, British forces stormed the city and the fort, killing hundreds of people. They demolished buildings in the fort and built huge barracks. Five decades later, the freedom movement gathered strength. In 1945, three members of the INA (Indian National Army) were tried by a British court in the fort and were eventually released. Independent India was born on 15 August 1947.

**SUNEHRI MASJID**
*Legend has it that Nadir Shah sat on the roof of the Sunehri Masjid (Golden Mosque) in Chandni Chowk, watching the destruction of the city.*

**INDEPENDENT INDIA**
*In August 1947, Jawaharlal Nehru, India's first prime minister, hoisted the national flag at the Red Fort ramparts. This has since become a tradition for every Independence Day.*

**SOOTHING AMBIENCE**
*The fading rays of the sun fall on the interior of the Rang Mahal in the evening, bathing the palace in a mellow light.*

## Mughal Architecture

Established in the 16th century, the Mughal empire grew rapidly to cover most of the Indian subcontinent. This was paralleled by the genesis of Mughal architecture, born out of a cohesive blend of Central Asian architectural styles with the indigenous forms. Mughal architecture is exemplified by Islamic elements such as calligraphy, intricately carved niches, domes, and pointed arches. The use of *chhajjas* (projecting eaves) reflects influences from Rajasthani architecture, while the curved roofs indicate a Bengali origin. Intricate inlay work and *jaalis* (perforated screens or latticed tracery) are common in Mughal buildings. The *charbagh* (quadrilateral garden layout further divided into four parts) originated in Persia. Shah Jahan's architectural style was typified by an increased use of marble and a gradual refinement in the ornamentation of buildings, such as inlaid semi-precious stones; cusped arches and foliated plinths were also extensively employed.

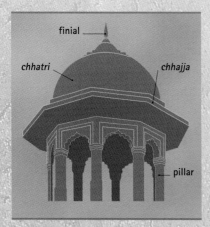

**⚜ CHHATRI**
*The* chhatri *(umbrella-shaped pavilion), adopted from Rajasthani architecture, is a common rooftop feature in Mughal buildings.*

finial
chhatri
chhajja
pillar

# Gateways

The structure of the gateways and their strategic location provided major defensive advantages. The occupants of the fort could regulate entry by lifting the drawbridges, and

defend themselves against enemies while hiding behind the parapets with large merlons (upward-projecting parts of a battlement). The giant bastions also strengthened the defence. Of the five existing gates, the two major ones are the massive Lahore and Delhi Gates.

**⚜ ADDITIONAL DEFENCE**
*In order to guard the Lahore Gate, Emperor Aurangzeb had a barbican (fortified outpost) built to the west side of the gate.*

merlon on parapet

barbican of Lahore Gate

# Delhi Gate

This gate, which forms part of the southern wall of the fort, faces the direction of the settlements that predated the Red Fort. Emperor Shah Jahan is said to have used this gate when he visited the Jama Masjid for Friday prayers. The Delhi Gate is protected by a barbican, while a pair of large stone elephants stand guard inside the gate.

**BARBICAN OF DELHI GATE**

# Lahore Gate

Called so because it faces Lahore (now in Pakistan), the Lahore Gate is a three-storeyed gateway set into the western wall of the Red Fort, and the fort's primary entrance. The pointed arch in the entrance is nested within another similar arch, which in turn forms a recessed sandstone façade. *Kanguras* (ornamental merlons) line the parapet above. Octagonal towers stand on the sides, capped with sandstone domes and marble finials. A series of indented niches adorn these towers.

**BRASS DESIGN** ✦
*Brass sheets were embossed onto the inner wooden doors to strengthen them.*

marble domes on *chhatris*

red stone pinnacle

**LAHORE GATE**

# Layout of the Red Fort complex

Constructed on the western bank of the river Yamuna, the Red Fort is a massive fort-palace complex that marks the northeastern corner of the medieval city of Shahjahanabad. Bastions at regular intervals further strengthen the outer wall and ramparts. *Chattris* and turrets line the wall. The fort is surrounded by a now dry moat. Public entry is through the Lahore Gate on the western side of the fort. The length of the fort is about 900m (2,953ft) from north to south and 550m (1,804ft) from east to west. The outer rampart walls traverse a perimeter of 2.41km (1.5 miles). The plan below highlights the areas of historical interest in the section accessible to the public.

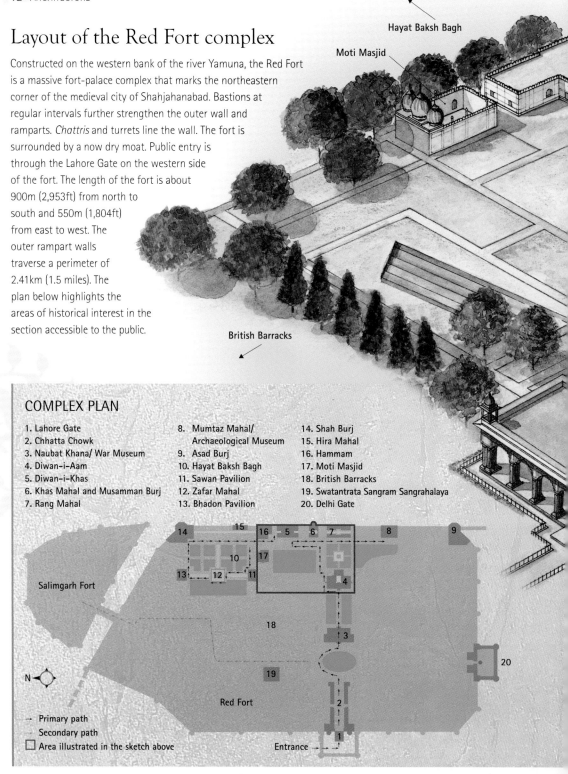

Hayat Baksh Bagh

Moti Masjid

British Barracks

## COMPLEX PLAN

1. Lahore Gate
2. Chhatta Chowk
3. Naubat Khana/ War Museum
4. Diwan-i-Aam
5. Diwan-i-Khas
6. Khas Mahal and Musamman Burj
7. Rang Mahal
8. Mumtaz Mahal/ Archaeological Museum
9. Asad Burj
10. Hayat Baksh Bagh
11. Sawan Pavilion
12. Zafar Mahal
13. Bhadon Pavilion
14. Shah Burj
15. Hira Mahal
16. Hammam
17. Moti Masjid
18. British Barracks
19. Swatantrata Sangram Sangrahalaya
20. Delhi Gate

Salimgarh Fort

N

Red Fort

→ Primary path
— Secondary path
☐ Area illustrated in the sketch above

Entrance →

---

Hammam

Diwan-i-Khas

Khas Mahal

Rang Mahal

Mumtaz Mahal

Diwan-i-Aam

North

## INNER PALACE COMPLEX

*The Diwan-i-Aam (Hall of Public Audiences) leads to the inner complex of the fort. Here stand the Rang Mahal (Palace of Colours), Khas Mahal (Emperor's Palace), Diwan-i-Khas (Hall of Private Audiences), Hammam (Bath House), and the Moti Masjid (Pearl Mosque).*

## MATERIALS

The Red Fort or Lal Qila (*lal* means "red" and *qila* means "fort") derives its name from the red sandstone, which is used as facing on the walls, covering the brick masonry. The sandstone was obtained from Fatehpur Sikri and from kingdoms around Delhi. White marble was brought in from the mines at Makrana in western India. Precious stones used in the inlay work on marble included diamonds, rubies, sapphires, emeralds, and pearls.

# Chhatta Chowk

The Lahore Gate leads to a vaulted arcade called the Chhatta Chowk (Roofed Arcade), which houses one of the covered bazaars of the 17th century. Divided into two parts by an octagonal courtyard in the middle, this two-storeyed arcade has 32 bays with cusped arches, which function as shops on the ground floor, like in the Mughal times. The upper floor sections are now barricaded.

**♥ IMPOSING ARCHWAY**
*The vaulted ceiling of Chhatta Chowk is supported by broad arches bearing patterns in stucco; these were once painted and gilded.*

**❦ ARABESQUE DESIGN**
*A series of geometric designs covers the ceiling, creating a pattern. It is a common element in Mughal architecture.*

**MEENA BAZAAR ❧**
*During the Mughal period, the shops in the marketplace used to sell brocades, velvets, silverware, spices, precious stones, and weapons. Today, the shops sell handicrafts, jewellery, textiles, antiques, and other goods.*

### HATHI POL
*It is said that only princes on their elephants were allowed to pass through the majestic Hathi Pol (Elephant Gate).*

**MOTIFS ON WALL**

# Naubat Khana

Further on from the bazaar is a three-storeyed sandstone pavilion called the Naubat Khana (Music Gallery). It is also referred to as the Naqqar Khana (Drum House) because this is where musicians played their instruments five times a day to announce prayers, on special occasions, and to herald the arrival of royalty. The instruments included drums, cymbals, trumpets, and the *shehnai* (an oboe-like woodwind instrument).

cusped window · recessed niche

### INDIAN WAR MEMORIAL MUSEUM
*The museum (on the second floor) contains exhibits of war-related objects such as body armour and weapons like swords, daggers, and shields. These are mainly from the Mughal era.*

### TRACERY WORK
*A stone arch set into the wall on the ground floor displays tracery work incorporating calligraphic inscriptions from Persian texts.*

### 🐾 HALL OF PUBLIC AUDIENCES
*The Diwan-i-Aam stands to the east of the Naubat Khana. The original courtyard in front has been replaced by lawns.*

## Diwan-i-Aam

Standing at the edge of the inner palace complex, the Diwan-i-Aam (Hall of Public Audiences) was the venue for the emperor's interactions with his subjects, who would fill the hall and the adjoining courtyard. It is said that the emperor routinely resolved disputes on the spot and inspected parades of soldiers and animals.

The pillars and ceiling of the hall were originally overlaid with gilded lime stucco, traces of which are still visible. The majestic façade comprises a nine-arched arcade supported on sandstone double columns.

underside
of arch
was gilded

cusp

### 💚 CARVINGS ON PLINTH
*These fine carvings on sandstone are a testament to the skill of the artisans of the Mughal age.*

### 🐚 ASSEMBLY HALL
*The roof of the main hall is supported by three parallel rows of columns that hold up a series of symmetrical, cusped arches.*

**⌓ CURVED ROOF ON PAVILION**
*Set in a niche in the wall at the centre of the front hall, the pavilion has a roof in the form of a curvilinear cornice; this is an adaptation of the sloping roof characteristic of Bengali architecture.*

## Marble pavilion

Profusely carved and embellished with precious stones, the marble pavilion (Nashiman-i-Zill-Ilahi or Seat of the Shadow of God) housed the emperor's throne, and is the focal point of the great hall. The inlay work on the wall behind the pavilion is attributed by some to the French jeweller, Austin de Bordeaux. Certain panels were removed after the First War of Independence, and were later restored. Steel rails bordering the pavilion have replaced the original ones, which were made of silver.

**FLORAL RELIEF ⌁**
*Flower clusters are set within intricate borders on the relief carvings that adorn the pavilion's platform. Makrana marble, sourced from the Nagaur district in present-day Rajasthan, was used to build the pavilion.*

### PIETRA DURA

The wall of the central recessed arch behind the pavilion is ornamented with pietra dura or inlay work. The marble panels were decorated with multi-coloured precious and semi-precious stones to enhance the naturalism in the rendering of birds, fruits, and floral motifs.

Greek god Orpheus playing the lute

**PATTERNS ON MARBLE**

floral inlay work on marble

**⌓ WAZIR'S DAIS**
*A marble dais supported by pillars stands in front of the pavilion. It was used by the wazir (prime minister) to submit public petitions to the emperor.*

# Diwan-i-Khas

Faced with polished marble, the Diwan-i-Khas (Hall of Private Audiences) stands atop a plinth. The scalloped arches are supported on a set of 32 columns with square shafts. Inscribed on the arches of the northern and southern walls of the Diwan-i-Khas is the famous Persian couplet: "*Agar Firdaus baru-i-zamin ast, hamin ast, hamin ast, hamin ast*" ("If there is paradise on Earth, it is this, it is this, it is this"). The Nahr-i-Bahisht (Canal of Paradise) was a channel of water that once flowed under this pavilion. The *Son-et-Lumière* (Sound and Light) show is held regularly in the ground in front of the hall and brings the history of Delhi and the Red Fort to life.

⚜ **OPULENT INTERIOR**
*The ceiling and walls of the chamber were embellished with silver, gold, and precious stones, before being plundered in the 18th and 19th centuries.*

❦ **HALL OF PRIVATE AUDIENCES**
*The Diwan-i-Khas is where the emperor received important guests like kings and ambassadors in private. The Khas Mahal (Emperor's Palace) adjoins the building.*

chhatri

⚜ **GILDED CAPITAL**
*The upper parts of the piers enclosing the central chamber, and the foliated arches that the piers gave rise to, were originally painted in gold.*

**FLORAL ARTISTRY** ❧
*Shah Jahan's artisans used precious and semi-precious stones to adorn the floral inlay work that can be seen all over the hall.*

⚜ **THRONE PEDESTAL**
*The marble pedestal on which the Takht-i-Taus was placed, originally stood at the centre of the hall. It is currently placed near the eastern wall.*

# Takht-i-Taus

More commonly known as the Peacock Throne (so called because of figures of two peacocks carved on the back of the throne), the Takht-i-Taus was placed in the central chamber of the Diwan-i-Khas and was used by the emperor on important state occasions. The throne was made of gold and studded with sapphires, emeralds, diamonds, pearls, and rubies. It was taken away by Nadir Shah of Persia when he plundered the fort in 1739. After his death, the throne was broken up. Some fragments were used in the throne that can be seen currently in the Golestan Palace in Iran.

engrailed arch

Khas Mahal

marble platform

⚜ **PLANTS ON MARBLE**
*Pietra dura work in the form of inlaid representations of foliage and flowers can be seen on the lower surface of the marble pillars.*

## KOH-I-NOOR

The most famous of the many precious stones in the Takht-i-Taus is a diamond called the *Koh-i-Noor* (Mountain of Light), which was embedded in the canopy of the throne. After many adventures, it is today a part of the British Crown jewels.

marble-clad dome

# Khas Mahal

A platform connects the Diwan-i-Khas with the Khas Mahal (Emperor's Palace or Special Palace), which contained the emperor's personal living quarters and is a composite structure consisting of three sections. The Tasbih Khana (Chamber for Prayer) and the Tosha Khana (Robe Chamber) flank the central room called the Khwabgah (Chamber of Dreams), which has marble screens on the northern and southern walls.

**THE EMPEROR'S PALACE**

### MIZAN-I-INSAF ⟩
*Resting within a crescent on the outer surface of the northern wall of the Khwabgah is the bas-relief called Mizan-i-Insaf (Scales of Justice), which was part of the emperor's insignia.*

### ❧ TASBIH KHANA
*The first chamber is made of three rooms and a triple-arched opening facing the Diwan-i-Khas. The plain lower surface of the walls contrasts with the upper half, which is ornamented with inlay work in indented niches.*

### ❧ ELEPHANT HEAD
*The doors on the wall flanking the Tasbih Khana are made of metal and are embellished with elephant-head brackets.*

⚜ **CEILING OF TOSHA KHANA**
*Traditional Mughal motifs seen on the ceiling were once adorned with silver and gold.*

# Musamman Burj

The Musamman Burj (Octagonal Tower) or the Burj-i-Tila (Golden Tower) is connected with the eastern wall of the Khwabgah in the Khas Mahal. The emperor used to appear at the window every morning, to be seen by his subjects standing below on the river-banks. A marble dome has replaced the original gilded copper dome.

MUSAMMAN BURJ

# Rang Mahal

This palace lies next to the Khas Mahal and was used as a residence by the queens and their hand-maidens. The women watched elephant matches of strength on the sandy banks of the Yamuna below from the grilled openings on the eastern wall. A lavishly decorated pillared structure, the palace has a central hall with small chambers opening out from its fifteen bays. The Rang Mahal (Palace of Colours) is constructed in marble and red sandstone, and the interior is adorned with delicate floral and foliage inlay work. Continuing from under the Khas Mahal, the water channel known as the Nahr-i-Bahisht flowed through the Rang Mahal into a lotus-shaped, marble fountain basin in the centre of the palace. Reflections of the inlay work would shimmer in the water of the channel and basin, heightening the beauty of the palace.

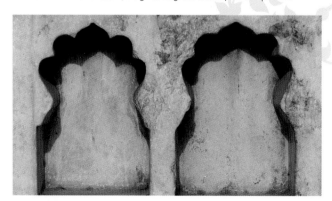

**MARBLE NICHES**

## ⚜ PALACE OF COLOURS
*The Rang Mahal derives its name from the original coloured ornamentation in the interior.*

## ⚜ COOLING DEVICES
*Small jaalis (lattice-work) on the wall functioned as natural ventilators, filtering in air to cool the interior of the palace.*

**⊛ SHEESH MAHAL**
*Four chambers on the northern and southern sides of the Rang Mahal have ceilings decorated with embossed glass mirrors, which is why each of these is called a Sheesh Mahal (Palace of Mirrors).*

**⊛ CENTRAL ARCHWAY**
*The northern end of the palace opens to a triple arch with marble columns and jaali or tracery work on top.*

# Mumtaz Mahal

Princesses lived in this palace named Mumtaz Mahal (Beautiful Palace). Cusped arches framing *jaalis* line the outer walls on the sides, and floral carvings are visible at the base of the walls. Marble pillars support arches in the hall within. The Rang Mahal and the Mumtaz Mahal formed the *zenana* (women's quarters). The Asad Burj, a tower at the southeastern end of the fort, can be seen from here.

**CARVINGS ON MARBLE**

**SANDSTONE JAALI**

**⊛ ARCHAEOLOGICAL MUSEUM**
*The palace is presently used by the ASI (Archaeological Survey of India) as a museum to display objects primarily from the Mughal era.*

# Hayat Baksh Bagh

A carefully planned garden complex, the Hayat Baksh Bagh (Life-Bestowing Garden) was made in the *charbagh* style (*char* means "four" and *bagh* means "garden"), a quadrilateral garden layout that originated in ancient Persia. This fourfold form comprised a garden intersected by a pair of channels or waterways at right angles. The point of intersection at the centre would usually be highlighted with a central pool, often with an accompanying pavilion.

BAHADUR SHAH ZAFAR'S PALACE

## BRITISH BARRACKS

The barracks were built by the British after the First War of Independence (when Indian sepoys arose in rebellion against the British forces) in 1857. Large portions of the Red Fort were destroyed at the time. Some sections of the barracks were constructed in the space that was once the Mehtab Bagh (Garden of Moonlight), and overlook the Hayat Baksh Bagh complex.

# Zafar Mahal

The Zafar Mahal (Zafar's Palace) is a sandstone pavilion built by Bahadur Shah Zafar, the last Mughal emperor. It is situated in the middle of the large tank at the centre of the Hayat Baksh Bagh. The palace has a courtyard in the centre with square rooms at the four corners. The plain architectural style contrasts with Shah Jahan's, which was ornamental in style and form.

🔹 **SANDSTONE ARCH**
*The Bhadon pavilion can be seen through an arched opening to the Zafar Mahal.*

barracks

**THE WATER SYSTEM**
*The pavilions are identical in design and formed part of the garden water system. Cascades of water flowed out from them and into the canal network, causing a cooling effect.*

DETAIL ON PILLAR CAPITAL

# Sawan and Bhadon pavilions

The Sawan pavilion is located at the southern end of the Hayat Baksh Bagh, while the Bhadon pavilion stands at the northern end. Sawan (derived from the Hindi word, *shravan*) and Bhadon denote the first two months of the rainy season, according to the Hindu calendar.

**NICHES FOR CANDLES**
*Candles would burn in these niches, behind a sheet of falling water. The niches are set in the bases of the pavilions, facing the garden.*

**HAYAT BAKSH BAGH**
*The Hayat Baksh Bagh adjoins the inner palace complex. The original canals converged at the central tank.*

**CARVED PILLARS**
*The 16 marble pillars in each of the pavilions are cylindrical in shape and have moulded bases.*

*The pavilion in front of the Shah Burj is capped by
a curved roof typical of Bengali architecture.*

marble incline
leading to basin

# Shah Burj

The Shah Burj (Royal Tower) is located at the northeastern corner of the Red
Fort. This was used by the emperor for his private meetings with his council,
which included courtiers, princes, and the *wazir* (prime
minister). Water from the Yamuna would be drawn into
the tower and then distributed to the rest of the fort.
The pavilion in the foreground is believed to have been
built by Emperor Aurangzeb.

NAHR-I-BAHISHT &#9752;
*The basin in front of the pavilion was where the
canal called Nahr-i-Bahisht (Canal of Paradise)
started from; it ran under the palaces and
pavilions, parallel to the eastern wall of the fort.*

**INLAY WORK**

# Hira Mahal

An elevated sandstone terrace runs along the
eastern wall of the fort between the Shah Burj
and the Hammam (Bath House). It was on this
terrace that Emperor Bahadur Shah Zafar built
the pavilion called the Hira Mahal (Diamond
Palace). Cusped arches and a plain marble parapet
can be seen on the minimally decorated sides.

**DIAMOND PALACE**

# Moti Masjid

Named after the pearly gloss of its marble, the Moti Masjid (Pearl Mosque) has high walls with embattled parapets. These surround the courtyard and can be seen through the latticed screen in the northern wall. *Mihrabs* (niches) have been carved into the west wall. The floor inside is decorated with black marble outlines of *musallas* (prayer mats).

**⚶ PEARL MOSQUE**
*The Moti Masjid was built in white marble by Emperor Aurangzeb and stands next to the Hayat Baksh Bagh.*

pinnacle

**MARBLE DOMES**

**COPPER–PLATED DOOR**

**⚶ BASINS FOR BATHS**
*Basins and tanks were provided for hot, cold, rose water, and vapour baths.*

# Hammam

The Ghusal Khana (*ghusal* means "wash" and *khana* means "a room") or the Hammam stands opposite the Moti Masjid. A series of pipes and tanks embedded in the walls and the ground supplied hot or cold water to the Hammam. The floor and walls of the chambers were decorated with gems and inlay work.

**⚶ SOUTHERN FAÇADE**
*Three cusped arches on the southern side face the Diwan-i-Khas. The central chamber is flanked by two smaller chambers; the channel where the Nahr-i-Bahisht flowed is visible at the centre.*

spandrel

## Shah Jahan's City

Shahjahanabad was not the first settlement but the seventh city (the others were Qila Rai Pithora, Mehrauli, Siri, Tughlaqabad, Firozabad, and Jahanpanah) in the region that became known as *Dilli* or Delhi. The foundations of Shahjahanabad were laid in 1638 by Emperor Shah Jahan, when he decided to shift his capital after 11 years of rule in Agra. The emperor formally moved his court into the Red Fort in 1648 and the new capital became the centre of Mughal power. The city was well fortified when it was built, but only sections of the wall survive. You can still see a few of the original city gates – the Kashmere Gate, Delhi Gate, Ajmeri Gate, and Turkman Gate. As the Mughal empire declined, the city fell prey to Nadir Shah, the Marathas (warriors from central India), and to the British, who took control of the city in the 19th century. Delhi became the British capital in 1911 and the city of New Delhi was built two decades later. If you want to experience the flavour of Shahjahanabad or Purani Dilli (Old Delhi) today, then wander in the narrow, winding alleys, bustling streets, and the crowded markets, to savour the appetizing aromas, admire the monuments, and marvel at this harmonious melange of the past and the present.

**⚑ KASHMERE GATE**
*Seen here in a photograph from 1865, the Kashmere Gate of the walled city faces Kashmir.*

# In and around Old Delhi

Every street in Shahjahanabad has a story to tell. Some of the interesting places to see are Zinat-ul Masjid (means "Most Beautiful of Mosques"), St James' Church (Delhi's oldest church), Sisganj Gurudwara (Sikh shrine), and the building that houses Dara Shikoh's library (Dara Shikoh was Shah Jahan's eldest son).

## Dilli Chalo Park

The land east of the fort has been renovated into the Dilli Chalo Park, which literally means "Let's Go To Delhi Park", and is a reference to INA leader, Subhas Chandra Bose's, call to his countrymen during the freedom struggle against British rule. It is a good vantage point to admire the fort's majesty.

# Chandni Chowk

Opposite the Lahore Gate of the Red Fort is Chandni Chowk (Moonlit Square), one of the oldest markets in Delhi. Built in 1648 by Shah Jahan's daughter, Jahanara Begum, it was Shahjahanabad's arterial boulevard and main commercial hub. Chandni Chowk had a canal that ran down the centre of the street. Some of the places to visit are the Fatehpuri Masjid (mosque at western end), Dariba Kalan (jewellery), Kinari Bazaar (accessories for weddings and festivals), Khari Baoli (spices), Chawri Bazaar (brass and copper products), and the Paranthewali Gali (renowned for its foodstalls).

**⚜ BUSTLING MARKETPLACE**
*The Digambar Jain Temple can be seen in the foreground of Chandni Chowk. Today, this maze of lanes contains shops selling street food, electronic goods, books, antiques, and more.*

# Salimgarh Fort

Salim Shah, son of Afghan king Sher Shah Suri, built the Salimgarh Fort in 1546. This fort is located to the northeast of the Red Fort and predates it. Emperor Aurangzeb used the

Salimgarh Fort as a prison, as did the British. The Swatantrata Sangram Sangrahalaya (Freedom Struggle Museum) is located on the way to the Salimgarh Fort and near the Naubat Khana.

**A RUIN IN THE FORT COMPLEX**

entrance to the
Salimgarh Fort

**⚜ HISTORIC LINK**
*Shah Jahan built the bridge that connects the two forts.*

# Sunehri Masjid

Situated to the west of the Delhi
Gate of the Red Fort is the Sunehri
Masjid (Golden Mosque), which
was built in 1751 by Mughal
queen, Nawab Qudsiya Begum.
The prayer hall of the mosque is
capped by three domes that were
originally gilded with copper.
Another Sunehri Masjid is located
in the Chandni Chowk.

**GOLDEN MOSQUE**

# Jama Masjid

This grand mosque was built on a rocky outcrop by Emperor Shah
Jahan. Located to the west of the Red Fort, the mosque is positioned
at the approximate centre of the city of Shahjahanabad. The mosque
is made of marble and sandstone and can be entered through the
three massive gateways to the south or north. The prayer hall is
surmounted by three black and white marble domes behind the great
central arch. These are flanked by tall minarets that overlook the vast
courtyard, where over 20,000 people can pray together at one time.

**ARCHED CORRIDOR**

❦ **CENTRAL POOL**
*The pool in the inner courtyard
is regularly used by the devotees
for ritual ablutions.*

three-tiered gateway

# Tourist information

**By Air:** International travellers can use the Indira Gandhi International (IGI) Airport. Travellers within India can avail of flights to and from the domestic terminal of the IGI Airport. For enquiries, visit www.delhi-tourism-india.com/delhi-info. **By Rail:** Delhi is connected to all cities in India by the Indian Railways. For enquiries, visit www.indianrail.gov.in. **By Road:** Delhi is connected to all cities in India by road. **To get to the Red Fort:** Autorickshaws, taxis, and luxury coaches are available for hire. For enquiries, visit www.delhitourism.nic.in.

# Visitor's checklist

The best time to visit Delhi is between October and March. The Red Fort is open to visitors from 10am to 6pm from Tuesday to Sunday. The entrance fee is Rs 10 per head for citizens of India and SAARC countries, and US $5 or Rs 250 for visitors from other countries. Photography is permitted in the fort, so do take your camera along. For updates on fees and timings, visit www.delhi-tourism-india.com/delhi-info.

Here are a few things you need to carry when travelling in India.

- Drinking water, torch, map or guidebook, mosquito repellent, loose change, sunblock
- First aid kit, medication for tropical diseases, such as diarrhoea, dysentery, and malaria; water purification tablets
- Light cotton clothes in summer; woollens in winter; hat, umbrella, or raincoat (in the monsooon season), easy-to-remove comfortable footwear
- Credit cards or travellers' cheques (optional)

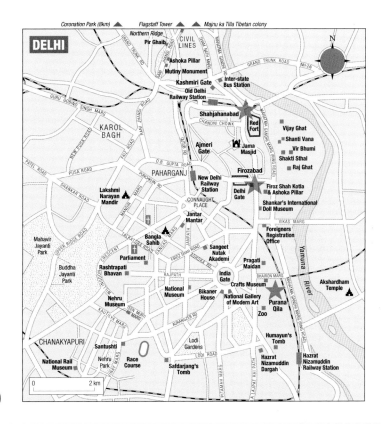

**Publisher's acknowledgements**

Dorling Kindersley and Penguin Books India would like to thank the following people for their help and guidance in preparing this book:
Dr Narayani Gupta and Ranjana Sengupta for reviewing the text so painstakingly; Punita Singh, Manager, Rough Guides India, for getting us permission to use the maps in the book; Jayaprakash Mishra of Rough Guides India and Suresh Kumar of DK Travel Guides for helping us with the maps.

**Picture credits**

The publishers are grateful to the following individuals, picture libraries, and companies for permission to reproduce their photographs.

**DK Images** 7bl, 7tl, 13br, 19br. **DK Travel Guides** 5c, 12/13c. **Rough Guides** 31cr. **Wikimedia Commons** (public domain) 28bl. **Amit Pasricha** 6bc. All other images by **Sanjay Austa.**

Abbreviations key: a=above, b=bottom, c=centre, f=far, l=left, t=top, r=right

Jacket Image: **Sanjay Austa.**

# Notes